D1809243

JACQUELYN YOUST

Grace and Gratitude

Your Fabulous Story

Copyright © 2020 by Jacquelyn Youst

All rights reserved. No part of this publication may be reproduced, stored or transmitted in any form or by any means, electronic, mechanical, photocopying, recording, scanning, or otherwise without written permission from the publisher. It is illegal to copy this book, post it to a website, or distribute it by any other means without permission.

First edition

This book was professionally typeset on Reedsy. Find out more at reedsy.com

Contents

Preface

Dear Friend,

You are about to embark on a journey of grace and gratitude! This is your opportunity to capture all the things you are grateful for, big and small.

Mix in a splash of grace and you will be surprised by the abundant joy you will experience daily. Grace and gratitude are a powerful combination. Together they will give you the inner peace and joy you deserve.

Take a moment to grab a cup of tea and smile. It's time to write your fabulous story.

With grace and gratitude,

Jacquelyn

One

Grace

Grace and Gratitude

Two

Gratitude

Grace and Gratitude

Three

Thankful

Grace and Gratitude

Four

The Little Things

Grace and Gratitude

Five

The Big Things

Grace and Gratitude

Six

Wishes

Grace and Gratitude

Seven

Surprises

Grace and Gratitude

Eight

Blessings

Grace and Gratitude

Nine

Inspirations

Grace and Gratitude

Ten

Prayers

Grace and Gratitude

Eleven

Hopes

Grace and Gratitude

Twelve

Kindness

Grace and Gratitude

Thirteen

Just Because

Grace and Gratitude

Fourteen

Positive Thoughts

Grace and Gratitude

Fifteen

Resolutions

Grace and Gratitude

Sixteen

Dreams

Grace and Gratitude

Seventeen

Happy Thoughts

Grace and Gratitude

Eighteen

Little Goals

Grace and Gratitude

Nineteen

Big Goals

Grace and Gratitude

Twenty

Random Thoughts

Grace and Gratitude

Twenty-One

More Random Thoughts

Grace and Gratitude

Twenty-Two

Joy

Grace and Gratitude

Twenty-Three

Pay it Forward

Lightning Source UK Ltd.
Milton Keynes UK
UKRC030442311221
396422UK00003B/139